638 1106

12/13

22.60

What Happens When I Cough?

By Benjamin Herbst

Gareth Stevens
Publishing

Please visit our website, www.garethstevens.com. For a free color catalog of all our high-quality books, call toll free 1-800-542-2595 or fax 1-877-542-2596.

Library of Congress Cataloging-in-Publication Data

Herbst, Benjamin
What happens when I cough? / Benjamin Herbst.
  p. cm. — (My body does strange stuff)
Includes index.
ISBN 978-1-4339-9334-3 (pbk.)
ISBN 978-1-4339-9335-0 (6-pack)
ISBN 978-1-4339-9333-6 (library binding)
1. Cough—Juvenile literature. 2. Reflexes—Juvenile literature. 3. Reflexes. I. Title
QP121.H531 2014
612.7—d23

Published in 2014 by
Gareth Stevens Publishing
111 East 14th Street, Suite 349
New York, NY 10003

Copyright © 2014 Gareth Stevens Publishing

Designer: Michael J. Flynn
Editor: Greg Roza

Photo credits: Cover, p. 1 © iStockphoto.com/VikramRaghuvanshi; p. 5 Zsolt, Biczô/ Shutterstock.com; p. 7 CLIPAREA|Custom media/Shutterstock.com; p. 9 Nuiiko/ Shutterstock.com; p. 11 AnneMS/Shutterstock.com; p. 13 Michael Krasowitz/ Photographer's Choice/Getty Images; p. 15 Martin Kucera/Shutterstock.com; p. 17 Chris Kruger/Shutterstock.com; p. 19 Maurizio Milanesio/Shutterstock.com.

Printed in the United States of America

CPSIA compliance information: Batch #CS13GS: For further information contact Gareth Stevens, New York, New York at 1-800-542-2595.

Contents

Boldface words appear in the glossary.

A Tickle in My Throat

When you're sick, you often cough a lot. You might also cough around smoke or when something is stuck in your throat. Coughing is a sign that something is wrong with your body. What causes us to cough? Let's find out!

5

Breathe In

When we breathe in, air enters our nose or mouth. It goes down a tube called the trachea (TRAY-kee-uh) and into our lungs. When something bothers the trachea, we cough to clear it out. A cough is a burst of air coming from the lungs.

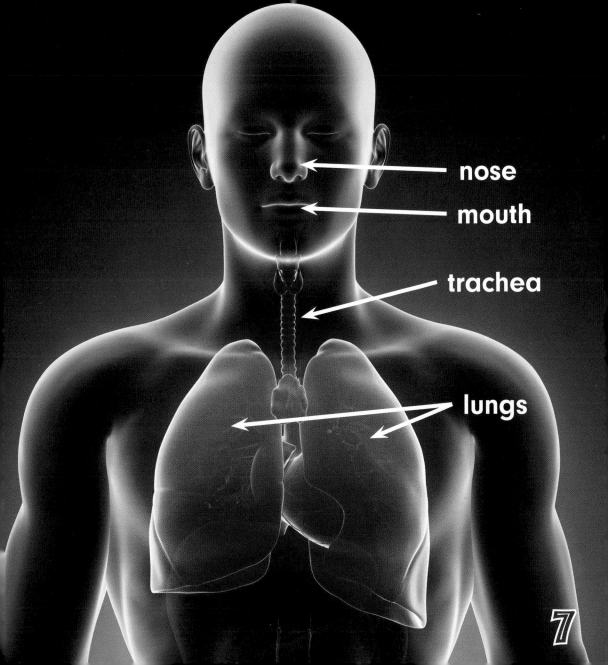

nose

mouth

trachea

lungs

7

Wrong Way!

Next to the trachea is a tube that leads to the stomach. Usually, a fold covers the top of the trachea when we eat. However, sometimes food goes into our trachea, and we can't breathe. We cough to force the food out.

Catch a Cold

When you're sick, your body makes extra **mucus** to fight **germs**. It drips from your nose into your throat. It may also build up in your lungs. Coughing is the body's way of clearing the mucus from your throat and lungs.

11

Sometimes when you're sick, your throat becomes sore and itchy. This can make you cough, too. It's important to cover your mouth when you cough, especially when you're sick. This keeps people around you from catching your cold.

Allergies

Someone with an allergy gets sick from things that don't bother other people—such as dust and pets. Allergies cause the body to make extra mucus. They can also cause the throat to feel itchy. These things can lead to coughing.

What Is Smoke?

Smoke is made when something burns. Smoke is made up of gases with very tiny **particles** floating in them. When people breathe in smoke, the particles bother the throat and lungs. This can cause you to cough.

Don't Smoke!

Cigarettes contain leaves called tobacco. They also contain many harmful **chemicals**. When someone breathes in cigarette smoke, tiny particles stay in the throat and lungs. This can cause coughing as well as other problems that are much worse.

Listen to Your Coughs

Sometimes we cough to clear our throat. However, a cough that won't go away is often a sign that something is wrong with your body. If you have a cough that you can't get rid of, you should go see a doctor.

mucus

sore throat

food in the trachea

colds

WHAT MAKES US COUGH?

allergies

smoke

mucus

itchy throat

21

Glossary

chemical: matter that can be mixed with other matter to cause changes

germ: a tiny creature that can cause illness

mucus: slimy stuff that keeps the inside of your body safe

particle: a very small piece of something

For More Information

Books

Durant, Penny. *Sniffles, Sneezes, Hiccups, and Coughs.* New York, NY: DK Publishing, 2005.

Larsen, C. S. *Crust & Spray: Gross Stuff in Your Eyes, Ears, Nose, and Throat.* Minneapolis, MN: Millbrook Press, 2010.

Powell, Jillian. *Coughs and Colds.* North Mankato, MN: Cherrytree Books, 2007.

Websites

KidsHealth
kidshealth.org/kid
Read more about coughing, colds, allergies, and many other health topics.

Smoking: The Smoking Scene
pbskids.org/itsmylife/body/smoking/index.html
Learn more about why smoking is bad for you.

Index